BUY THE ROSES BOOK THE TRIP SAY THE WORDS

A NO-REGRETS JOURNAL FOR PURE HAPPINESS

LUCY JUÁREZ

CASTLE POINT BOOKS
NEW YORK

Printed in the United States of America. For information,
address St. Martin's Press, 120 Broadway, New York, NY 10271.

www.castlepointbooks.com

The Castle Point Books trademark is owned by Castle Point Publishing, LLC.
Castle Point books are published and distributed by St. Martin's Publishing Group.

ISBN 978-1-250-27780-0 (paper-over-board)

Illustrations by AliRae Aguirre

First Edition: 2021

10 9 8 7 6 5 4 3 2 1

This journal belongs to:

____

LIVE,
TRAVEL,
ADVENTURE,
BLESS,
AND DON'T
BE SORRY.

–Jack Kerouac

INTRODUCTION

• • • • • •

TODAY IS THE DAY you begin painting your life with bold swaths of passion—celebrating each day as the new gift it is. From your wardrobe to your walls and your passport to your relationships, stop playing it safe and give yourself permission to pursue the desires of your heart. Wear the sequins. Paint it fuchsia. Go on that adventure. Say the words you've been afraid to voice.

Every page of this journal will encourage you to take chances, release fears, and live your life with no regrets. Whether you approach the pages one at a time or find the page that calls to you each day, inspiring words and journaling prompts will help you see clearly where your happiness lies and bring you closer to making your dreams a reality.

Buy the Roses, Book the Trip, Say the Words is your reminder to kiss your life "good morning" and throw your arms around the world. Enjoy the adventure in every day!

I PUT ON THE CANVAS WHATEVER COMES INTO MY MIND.

–*Frida Kahlo*

CREATE THE DAY

Think of today as your blank canvas, then fill the space below with how you want the hours ahead to come alive. At the end of the day, consider returning to this page and adding in the unexpected moments of joy that popped in as well.

I WISH TO
LIVE A LIFE
THAT CAUSES
MY SOUL
TO DANCE
INSIDE
MY BODY.

–*Dele Olanubi*

SATISFY YOUR SOUL

What skill completely unrelated to your career and family roles have you always wanted to learn? Whether it's riding a unicycle or watercolor painting, promise yourself here that you will pursue it (no more excuses!), and form a plan to make it happen.

Don't wait for someone to bring you flowers. Plant your own garden and decorate your own soul.

–Luther Burbank

BUY THE ROSES

Whose approval or affection are you waiting for? Write the name on the tag below, then cross it out and replace it with your own. To celebrate moving forward in your own confidence, buy yourself a bouquet of flowers and post a picture of the blooms here as a reminder of all you deserve simply for being who you are.

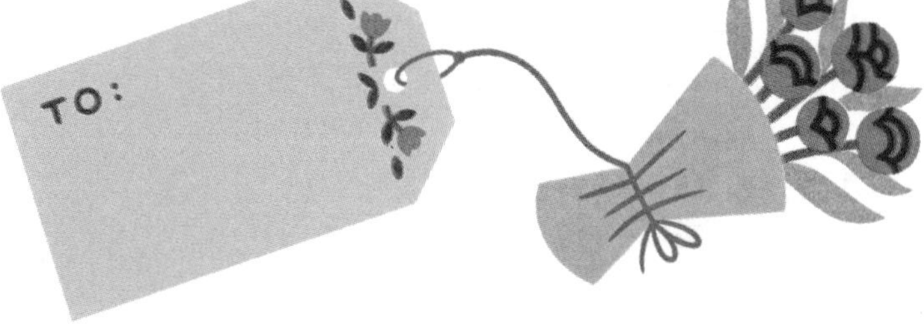

If you
obey all
the rules,
you'll miss
all the fun.

–Katharine Hepburn

BREAK THE RULES

What rule in your life—real or self-imposed—is holding you back from happiness? How will you break it in the name of unbridled joy?

You will
love me later
BECAUSE
I told you
the truth.

–Mary J. Blige

SAY THE WORDS

Call to mind someone you've been eager to reach on a deeper level. As you envision his or her face, boldly write below the words you want to say.

SET A TIME AND PLACE
to say the words face-to-face.

LET'S ENJOY THIS FLEETING MOMENT OF LIFE.

–*Omar Khayyam*

CELEBRATE THE NOW

Break out the champagne glasses for your orange juice. Wear those sequins on your errands. In what seemingly flamboyant ways can you celebrate this gift of a fresh day?

EACH CONTACT
WITH A
HUMAN BEING
IS SO RARE,
SO PRECIOUS,
ONE SHOULD
PRESERVE IT.

–Anaïs Nin

REACH OUT WITHOUT A REASON

When someone crosses your mind or heart today, don't stop and wonder why. Simply and spontaneously connect with them in person, by phone, or by text—no reason needed. Take it as a sign that you need them or they need you. What is the response?

THE

POETRY
OF EARTH
IS NEVER
DEAD.

–John Keats

LIVE IN FRESH AIR

Whenever you feel like you're at a stagnant point, come alive outdoors. Is there a place nearby where you can find lush growth, moving water, or changing seasons today—even if it's just for a moment during your usual comings and goings? Sketch a picture of the natural beauty you hope to find, then jot down how you feel after you have visited.

I must
keep to my
own style
and go
on in my
own way.

–Jane Austen

OWN YOUR STYLE

Think of a décor statement piece that makes you smile, even if others consider it tacky or over-the-top. A Christmas tree that stays up year-round? A collection of cat statues? Macramé to the extreme? If you own it now, where can you move it so that it's front and center in your home? If it's been stuck on your wish list, make a plan to purchase it and give it a place of honor.

ALL GOOD
THINGS
ARE WILD
AND FREE.
–Henry David Thoreau

GET WILD, CHILD

Find a photo of yourself as a child in whatever "wild" mode was for you growing up—whether you were creating your own version of a mud run or simply had wild hair that day. Post the picture here, then promise yourself a few ways to enjoy that devil-may-care spirit again.

Always dare to be in the company of those stronger than you.

–Israelmore Ayivor

GRAB A RUNG

Think of someone you've always admired. It could be for their career achievements, for making the world a better place, or just for how they interact with others and find balance in their daily life. How can you connect with this person, and what guidance or inspiration would you ask for?

I HAVEN'T BEEN EVERYWHERE, BUT IT'S ON MY LIST.

–Susan Sontag

BOOK THE TRIP

There's not always a convenient time to travel, and maybe that's the point. Traveling can push you out of your comfort zone and open your eyes to new perspectives. Whether it's across the state or around the world, mark three places you will travel to on the map below—ranking them in order from 1 (soonest) to 3 (last). Then commit to taking your first steps to make it happen.

First steps:

FOR NOW,
IT'S JUST YOU,
THE WORLD,
AND THE
SUNRISE.

–Unknown

EMBRACE THE MORNING

What will help you open your bright eyes and jump out of bed into the day—and all the possibilities it holds? Plan a few simple ways to invite joy and spirit into the first moments of your day.

Wake-up song or alarm sound:

First sights to place within view (a plant or fresh flowers, a favorite photo, a special memento?):

What I want to do before my feet even hit the floor (stretch, meditate, pray, envision a wonderful day?):

The first move I will make:

Life must be aromatic.

THERE MUST BE SCENT,

somehow there must be some.

—Gwendolyn Brooks

BREATHE IN BEAUTY

Do you long to breathe in the salty ocean air, surround yourself with the aroma of freshly ground coffee or freshly baked bread, or walk among floral scents in a greenhouse or garden? Allow your sense of smell to lead you somewhere not on your schedule today. How does the experience awaken your day?

To get the full value of joy you must have someone to divide it with.

–Mark Twain

SET A DATE

How many times have you said, "We should get together"? Choose two people to whom you've spoken those words and actually meant it. Reach out to them today to set a date, time, and place to follow through.

Get together with	*Get together with*
Date/time:	*Date/time:*
Place:	*Place:*
What I'm looking forward to:	*What I'm looking forward to:*

ALWAYS BE THIRSTY FOR LIFE; ALWAYS BE HUNGRY FOR LOVE.

–Debasish Mridha

DRINK IN LIFE

What are you thirsty for more of in your everyday life? Circle the words that resonate with you, or add some of your own.

ADVENTURE

SPONTANEITY

CONNECTION

CREATIVITY

PASSION

FRESH AIR

NEW EXPERIENCES

What steps can you take this week to quench that thirst?

When the voice of self-doubt gets loud, remember you control the volume.

–Unknown

TURN UP THE VOLUME

What areas of your life would it feel good to amplify? Circle the words that resonate with you, or add some of your own.

MUSIC
MY OWN VOICE
ENCOURAGING VOICES OF OTHERS
CONFIDENCE
INTUITION
PURPOSE
BRAVERY

What steps can you take this week to nudge that dial?

Immerse yourself in **BEAUTY** *and bathe yourself in* **POSITIVITY.**

–Charlie Grant

DIVE IN DEEP

In what can you immerse yourself to fuel your days with more passion? Circle the words that resonate with you, or add some of your own.

WATER

POETRY

ART

NATURE

LIVE MUSIC OR EVENTS

LEARNING NEW SKILLS

SOCIALIZING

What steps can you take this week to saturate your life?

Cooking is like love. It should be entered into WITH abandon or not at all.

–Harriet Van Horne

AIM FOR ABANDON

Make a list of three things you currently do with abandon. It could be anything: run, paint, love, cook, play an instrument, etc. Add three more things you would like to start doing with more passion. After you create the list, choose one to enjoy today.

Now

1.

2.

3.

Goals

1.

2.

3.

YOU'VE GOT
TO JUMP
OFF CLIFFS
ALL THE TIME
AND BUILD
YOUR WINGS
ON THE WAY
DOWN.

—*Annie Dillard*

STEP OUT FOR ANOTHER

Not all the risks we take in life only benefit ourselves. Who can you take a risk for this week to support their no-regrets life?

MUSIC IS THE DIVINE WAY TO TELL BEAUTIFUL, POETIC THINGS TO THE HEART.

–Pablo Casals

SERENADE YOUR SPIRIT

Create an eclectic playlist. The only thread that needs to run between all of the songs is that they make you feel alive and inspired.

Always serve
TOO MUCH
hot fudge sauce
on hot fudge
sundaes. It
makes people
OVERJOYED
and puts them
in your debt.

–Judith Olney

BE TOO MUCH

Extravagant love and giving are great aims for living with passion. What can you do that will make someone say, "You're too much!" in a good way?

REMEMBER, THE

talking about

THE THING

ISN'T THE THING.

Doing the thing

IS THE THING.

–Amy Poehler

STOP THE TALKING

Name three things you just can't stop talking about lately.

1.

2.

3.

Now go back and turn them into actions you can take beyond just talk.

HOW WE HANDLE
OUR FEARS
WILL DETERMINE
WHERE WE GO
WITH THE REST
OF OUR LIVES.
TO EXPERIENCE
ADVENTURE OR
TO BE LIMITED BY
THE FEAR OF IT.

–Judy Blume

FACE YOUR FEARS

Fears can hold us captive in a cycle of living life small. List three fears below in the order you're committed to tackling them. Next to each, write down a plan for how you can approach each one.

Fear	*How to Face*
1.	
2.	
3.	

The more
you praise
and celebrate
your life,
the more
there is in life
to celebrate.

–Oprah Winfrey

MARK MORE DAYS

From National Chocolate Covered Cherry Day (January 3) to National Name Your Car Day (October 2), you can find days that other people or organizations have created to celebrate throughout the year. But it's better to create your own. Mark your calendar with a true-to-you reason to celebrate at least once for each season—whether it's the day you brought home your pet or the day someone you love got an all-clear health report.

Spring celebration

Date:

Meaning behind:

How I'll celebrate:

Fall celebration

Date:

Meaning behind:

How I'll celebrate:

Summer celebration

Date:

Meaning behind:

How I'll celebrate:

Winter celebration

Date:

Meaning behind:

How I'll celebrate:

STRAIGHT
LINES GO
TOO QUICKLY
TO APPRECIATE
THE PLEASURES
OF THE JOURNEY.

–René Crevel

TAKE A DETOUR

It's easy to get stuck in a rut, but it can be just as easy to shake up some little paces in your day to find rewards. What detours from your usual routine can you take today? Consider things as simple as trying a different coffee shop or listening to new music.

The usual:

New turn:

How it felt:

The usual:

New turn:

How it felt:

LIFE IS A COMBINATION OF MAGIC AND PASTA.

—*Federico Fellini*

SCATTER THAT MAGIC

What feels like magic to you, even if you can't explain why? Cover this page with what instantly comes to mind, then aim to work as much of this magic into your week as you can.

WE CAN ONLY
BE SAID TO BE
ALIVE IN THOSE
MOMENTS WHEN
our hearts
are conscious
OF OUR
TREASURES.

–Thornton Wilder

POUR ON GRATITUDE

Don't hesitate or hold back on the sincere thank-yous. Notice and express gratitude for all of the people in your life who help you—in big or small ways—throughout the day. Note a few below and describe how they made your day brighter.

LIFE IS
A SEA OF
VIBRANT
COLOR.
JUMP IN.

–*A. D. Posey*

ADD A COLOR BURST

Think about what color makes you feel fabulous. How can you invite more of it into your life, whether it's into your wardrobe, onto your walls, or via a new tattoo or hair color? Sketch your colorful ideas below, then take the first steps to bring them to life.

There's something liberating about not pretending. Dare to embarrass yourself.

—Drew Barrymore

REVEAL YOUR TRUE SELF

What don't most people know about you that you are working up the courage to reveal? How can you share your story in a way that's brave yet safe?

Surprise is THE greatest gift which life can grant us.

–Boris Pasternak

PULL OFF A SURPRISE

Plan a party. Show up on someone's doorstep unannounced. Take your friends or family on a surprise trip. What surprise—big or small—will you choose and begin planning today to make happen?

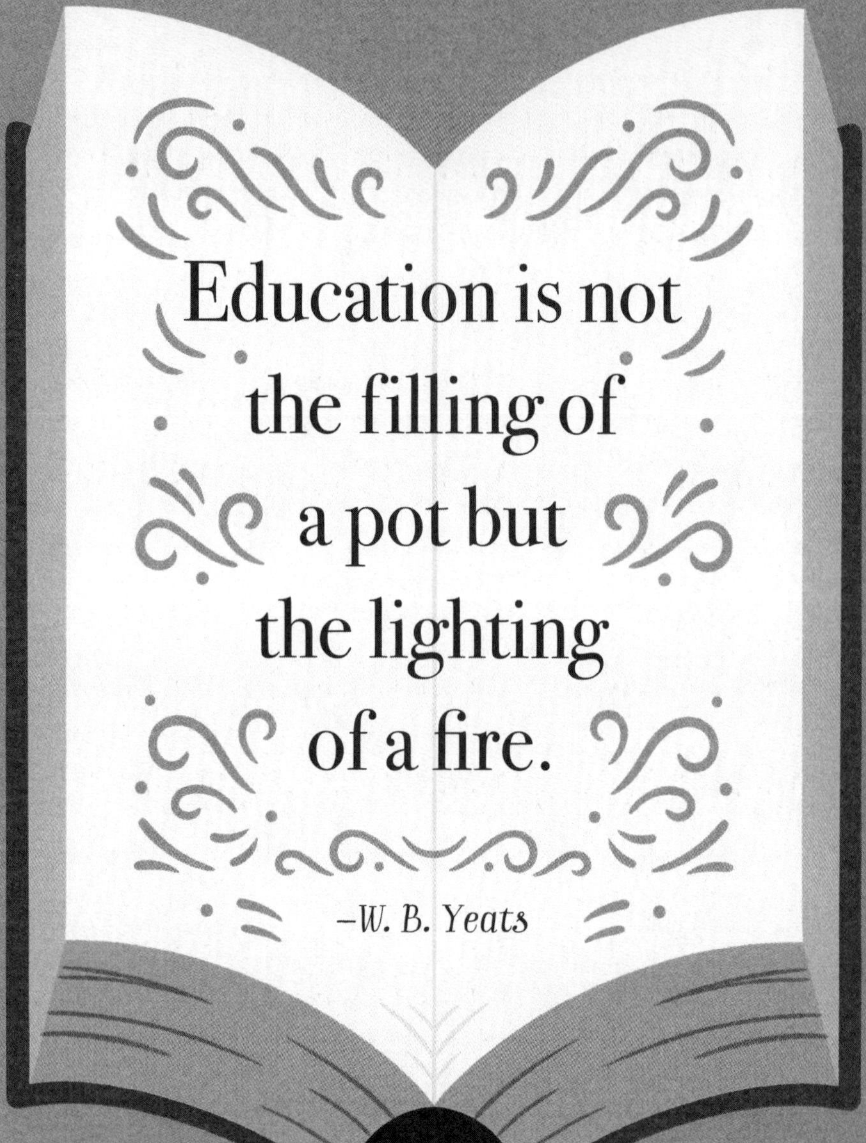
Education is not
the filling of
a pot but
the lighting
of a fire.
–W. B. Yeats

TEACH A SKILL

Whether you teach an ongoing class, give a one-time speech, or simply help a friend one-on-one, sharing a talent can help boost your confidence and allows you to spend time immersed in a world you love. What will you share and in what venue?

Wherever
you go,
go with all
your heart.

–*Confucius*

END THE WAIT

Where do you feel like you're caught in a waiting room in your life? How can you push to open the door to the main event?

LIFE'S TOO SHORT TO WEAR BORING CLOTHES.

—Carly Cushnie and Michelle Ochs

WEAR IT WELL

What fashion trend catches your eye but you've never indulged in because of the inner voice that says, "I couldn't pull that off"? Today is the day to silence that voice and wear what makes you happy—whether it's leather, crazy prints, or retro bell-bottoms. Sketch the "scandalous" attire you plan to wear here, then post a photo of you wearing it with your brightest smile.

SINCE YOU GET MORE JOY OUT OF GIVING JOY TO OTHERS, YOU SHOULD PUT A GOOD DEAL OF THOUGHT INTO THE HAPPINESS THAT YOU ARE ABLE TO GIVE.

–*Eleanor Roosevelt*

FILL A NEED

Keep your eyes and ears open today for someone who truly needs something you can easily give. Maybe a connection on your social feed is requesting donations for a charity or a coworker needs a dog-sitter so they can attend a funeral in another state. If the need is something you can fill, especially with little burden to yourself, don't hesitate. What can you say yes to?

The breath of life is
IN THE SUNLIGHT
and the hand of life
IS IN THE WIND.

—Kahlil Gibran

FEEL THE WIND

Drive with the windows down. Walk along a pier or open field. Get that bike out of the garage. Where can you feel the awakening of the wind today, and what does it spark in you?

IT'S ONLY BY SAYING NO THAT YOU CAN CONCENTRATE ON THE THINGS THAT ARE REALLY IMPORTANT.

–Steve Jobs

SKIP A TRADITION

While there's so much in life to shout yes about, sometimes the bravest moves require saying no. Think of a tradition or routine in your life that started as a good idea but now just feels like a burden. How can you let it go and free space for more of what you need and enjoy?

WRITE
AND DRAW
AND BUILD
AND PLAY
AND DANCE
AND LIVE
AS ONLY
YOU CAN.

–Neil Gaiman

BELT IT OUT

Whether it's crooning karaoke at the local dive bar, being the first to start singing "Happy Birthday" for a coworker, or simply not hiding your concert in the car, go big and go strong. What's the craziest singing session you've ever had or plan to participate in?

I can't bear living in this huge beautiful world and not try to imitate it as best I can.

–David Mitchell

SEE MORE WONDERS

The world is filled with so much magnificence! Make a list of ten specific sights, near or far, that you'd like to see. Put a star next to one you can make happen soon.

1.

2.

3.

4.

5.

6.

7.

8.

9.

10.

Where there is love AND inspiration, I don't think you can go wrong.

–*Ella Fitzgerald*

FIND YOUR TEAM

Who inspires spontaneity and adventure in you? Find and secure below a photo of yourself with at least one other person in which you're doing something crazy—whatever that looks like for you. Recall the freedom you felt in that moment. How can you spend more time together?

We don't stop playing because we grow old; we grow old because we stop playing.

–*George Bernard Shaw*

RELEASE YOUR INNER CHILD

Jump in the leaves. Pump your legs on a swing. Ask to pet every dog you cross paths with. Aim to fill your day with ten moments of play like no one is watching. What do you do?

1.

2.

3.

4.

5.

6.

7.

8.

9.

10.

LOOK AT EVERYTHING

in the world as if you are seeing it for the first time, and

PAINT EVERYTHING

as if you were seeing it for the last time.

–Andrew Hamilton

PAINT A PICTURE

Step away from painting parties with prescribed subjects. Find something that truly moves you and put it on canvas in a way you can appreciate—whether it's a pretty accurate representation or simply splashes of color that reflect emotions. Display it somewhere, anywhere, then describe what you've created and the experience of creating it below.

IF WE WERE MEANT TO STAY IN ONE PLACE, WE'D HAVE ROOTS INSTEAD OF FEET.

–Rachel Wolchin

DARE TO MOVE

What's the biggest physical move you've ever made—relocating, walking across a crowded room to meet someone, running a race, climbing a steep trail or mountain? You can measure "big" in terms of distance or courage.

What's the next big move you're planning?

THE
DISCOVERY
OF A NEW DISH
DOES MORE
FOR HUMAN
HAPPINESS
THAN THE
DISCOVERY OF
A NEW STAR.

–Jean Anthelme
Brillat-Savarin

EXPAND YOUR PALATE

Make a list of all the foods you'd like to try in the next year. Then aim to explore a few new tastes each month. Come back and cross out the ones you wouldn't enjoy again and put a star next to those you're glad you discovered.

Never be afraid to raise your voice for honesty and truth and compassion.

–William Faulkner

“ LIFT YOUR VOICE ”

Whether your style is more protesting in the streets or starting a petition, choose an issue that matters to you and give your time and voice to it in the next week. Where can you make a difference?

IT'S ONE THING
TO MAKE A
PICTURE OF WHAT
A PERSON LOOKS
LIKE, IT'S
ANOTHER THING
TO MAKE A
PORTRAIT OF
WHO THEY ARE.

–Paul Caponigro

• • • GET PRO PHOTOS • • •

It's a great feeling to have a photo you feel good about. If you shy away from having your picture taken or critique photos of yourself in secret later, hire a professional photographer (or photography student) to photograph you in an environment you're comfortable in. Splurge on hair and makeup, too, if you can. Plan the shoot below (who, where, when, what you'll wear), then post the beautiful results.

Live as if you were to die tomorrow. Learn as if you were to live forever.

—Mahatma Gandhi

ADMIT YOU DON'T KNOW

Knowledge is a gift you could miss out on if you aren't brave enough to say those three little words: "I don't know." What are three areas that you need to risk admitting your lack of knowledge about so you can be rewarded with new learning?

1.

2.

3.

FREEDOM IS THE OXYGEN OF THE SOUL.

–*Moshe Dayan*

LEAVE THE SCREEN

Choose at least one day each week when you stay away from screens. How much time and freedom does it feel like you discovered at the end of the day—and what did you do with the gains?

Twenty years from now you will BE more disappointed by the things that you didn't do than BY the ones you did do.

–Mark Twain

MAKE A CASE

What do you want in your life that you haven't asked for: a new job, a promotion, a dinner date, coffee with an expert in your field or area of interest? Target one opportunity that you will take the first step to go after this week.

Splurge on the most classic item in the world, and splurge on the most insane thing in the world. You will have and cherish them both forever.

–Isaac Mizrahi

GO AHEAD, SPLURGE

As long as it's not an everyday occurrence, you deserve to splurge every once in a while. Let your heart lead you to one classic splurge (pricey jeans, top-of-the-line kitchen knives, lux-thread-count sheets), and one crazier splurge (backstage passes, a hot-air balloon ride, Botox). What's your pleasure?

Classic

Crazy

HE WHO CAN NO LONGER PAUSE TO WONDER AND STAND RAPT IN AWE, IS AS GOOD AS DEAD; HIS EYES ARE CLOSED.

—Albert Einstein

FIND AWE AROUND YOU

Consider what never ceases to amaze you—perhaps a symphony of birdsong, a mountain's vast peaks, the way a loved one's eyes light up when they smile. Illustrate below (with words, drawings, or photos) what sparks awe in you.

You only get one chance at life and you have to grab it boldly.

–Bear Grylls

GRAB THE RING

If you've ever ridden an old-fashioned carousel, you know the magical feeling of grabbing the brass ring. Tangible joy is true and good. What five treasures can you reach for and hold in your hands today? Ideas to get you started: a loved one's hand, your favorite candy, a beloved book...

1.

2.

3.

4.

5.

Set your heights more than what you see around you, see beyond.

–Anthony Anderson

SEE NEW HEIGHTS

Go to a place that makes you feel like you're on top of the world. Will you climb a mountain, drive to a vantage point, fly in a helicopter, go for skydiving lessons, or take in the view from the top of a skyscraper? Make a plan, then post the view below.

It's your place
in the world;
it's your life.
Go on and do
all you can with
it, and make
it the life you
want to live.

–*Mae Jemison*

CUSTOMIZE YOUR TOPPINGS

Imagine your life as a pizza. Fill in the base slices that are important to you, then sprinkle them with the toppings that bring excitement and joy into your life.

Her intuition was
HER FAVORITE
superpower.

–*Unknown*

★★ FOLLOW THE NUDGES ★★

Live a day where you listen for that inner voice nudging you in certain directions and actually follow it. What unexpected discoveries, joys, and adventures did your intuition lead you to?

Make a
mark on
the world
that can't
BE erased.

–Maya Angelou

MAKE YOUR MARK

It's natural to want to live a memorable life. If you had to choose one "mark" for people to remember you by, what would it be?

Our body is precious.
It is our vehicle for awakening.

–Buddha

REACH A PHYSICAL GOAL

Whether you possess any athletic gifts or not, you can appreciate even the little things your body can do. Set a physical goal that's achievable for you, with some mini-milestones worked in, move toward it at your own pace, then celebrate your success.

Goal:

Milestones along the way:

Timetable to achieve:

How I'll celebrate:

We're the fullest when we're a tool that helps others grow.

–Unknown

HELP SOMETHING GROW

Whether you nurture a houseplant, an entire garden, a pet, a youth sports team with a dream, or a Little Sister or Little Brother, there is something big and bold and life changing about helping something—or someone—outside ourselves to grow. What or who can you support?

SOMETIMES WALKING AWAY HAS NOTHING TO DO WITH WEAKNESS, AND EVERYTHING TO DO WITH STRENGTH.

–*Robert Tew*

WALK AWAY STRONGER

It's so tempting to fight to be right or to have the last word, but sometimes it takes a lot more guts to just let it be. In what situation in your life right now can you resolve to be strong and just walk away?

One cannot think well, love well, sleep well, if one has not dined well.

–*Virginia Woolf*

DINE IN LUXURY

Treat yourself to an amazing dinner this week—no matter how busy your schedule is. Whether you choose to dine at home or out on the town, think beyond simply the food and drink to the entire experience and what will fill you with joy.

On the menu:

I will raise a toast to...

Finishing touches (maybe, outdoor seating at a restaurant or candles and music at home):

Alone or with a special companion?

DO NOT DARE NOT TO DARE.

—C. S. Lewis

• ✳ ◆ TAKE THE LEAP ◆ ✳ •

Cover this page with all of the risks—big and small—
you've taken in the past year that have paid off.

•• *What's the next leap you'll take?* ••

She loved life and it loved her right back.

–*Unknown*